SNEAKY PRESS
©Copyright 2022
Pauline Malkoun

The right of Pauline Malkoun to be identified as author of this work has been asserted by them in accordance with Copyright, Designs and Patents Act 1988.

All Rights Reserved.

No reproduction, copy or transmission of this publication may be made without written permission. No paragraph of this publication may be reproduced, copied or transmitted save with the written permission of the publisher, or in accordance with the provisions of the Copyright Act 1956 (as amended).

Any person who commits any unauthorized act in relation to this publication may be liable to criminal prosecution and civil claims for damages.

A catalogue record for this work is available from the National Library of Australia.

ISBN 9781922641267

Sneaky Press is the imprint of Sneaky Universe.
www.sneakyuniverse.com
First published in 2022

Sneaky Press
Melbourne, Australia.

Sneaky Jokes

Volume 2

Sneaky Press

Why are jokes great?

There are so many reasons that jokes are fabulous including the following:

⇒ Better overall health and wellbeing. Laughter is the best medicine — that's why there are clown doctors who treat sick children in hospitals.

⇒ Jokes provide opportunities to interact with others, building social skills.

⇒ Jokes help build literacy — reading, speaking, expanding vocabulary, identifying sounds, additional meanings and spelling.

⇒ Jokes help build coping skills. They give us an outlet when we are faced with a tough situation — laughing at a joke can help relieve stress.

Why couldn't Cinderella play soccer?

Because she always ran away from the ball.

What do cows like to read?

CATTLE-logs.

What do you call a fly that doesn't have wings?

A walk!

Can a kangaroo jump higher than a tree?

Of course! Trees can't jump!

Why did the barber win the race?

He knew a shortcut.

What did one hat say to the other hat?

"Stay here, I'm going on a head."

How do modern-day pirates keep in touch?

SEA-mail.

Where do horses live?

In neighhh-bourhoods.

What do you get when you put cheese next to some ducks?

Cheese and quackers.

Why did the Scottish man have plumbing issues?

He only had bagpipes.

Have you heard the rumour about butter?

Never mind, I shouldn't be spreading it.

What did the buffalo say when his son left?

"Bi-son!"

I used to be addicted to the hokey pokey...

But then I turned myself around.

Why did the actor fall through the floorboards?

He was just going through a stage.

Why don't scientists trust atoms?

Because they make up everything!

What do you call a parade of rabbits hopping backward?

A receding hare-line.

What did the shark say when he ate the clownfish?

"This tastes a little funny."

Why can't a tyrannosaurus clap?

It's extinct!

What do you call an elephant in a phone booth?

Stuck!

What do you call a blind dinosaur?

A Doyouthinkhesawus.

What do you call a dinosaur that does not take a bath?

A Stink-o-Saurus.

Why do fish live in salt water?

Because pepper makes them sneeze!

Knock knock.

Who's there?
Interrupting cow.

Interr...
MOO!!

What do you call a deer with no eyes?

No eye deer

Why did the fastest cat in school get suspended?

Because he was a cheetah.

Knock Knock
Who's there?
Who.

Who who?
Is there an owl in here?

Why is 6 terrified of 7?

Because 7 "8" 9!

What did one eye say to the other eye?

Don't look now, but there is something between us that smells.

What's brown and sticky?

A stick!

Two cookies were in the oven. One says, "It sure is hot in here!"

The other one says, "Holy smokes! A talking cookie!"

www.ingramcontent.com/pod-product-compliance
Lightning Source LLC
Chambersburg PA
CBHW042000080526
44588CB00021B/2816